"This generation of Christians inhabit cultures that sometimes reject not only biblical revelation about reality, but also the reality of reality itself. The Questions for Restless Minds series poses many of the toughest questions faced by young Christians to some of the world's foremost Christian thinkers and leaders. Along the way, this series seeks to help the Christian next generation to learn how to think biblically when they face questions in years to come that perhaps no one yet sees coming."

—Russell Moore,

public theologian, *Christianity Today*

"If you're hungry to go deeper in your faith, wrestle with hard questions, and are dissatisfied with the shallow content on your social media newsfeed, you'll really appreciate this series of thoughtful deep dives on critically important topics like faith, the Bible, friendship, sexuality, philosophy, and more. As you engage with some world-class Christian scholars, you'll be encouraged, equipped, challenged, and above all invited to love God more with your heart, soul, mind, and strength."

Andy Kim,

multiethnic resource director, InterVarsity Christian Fellowship

Who Chose the Books of the New Testament?

Questions for Restless Minds

Questions for Restless Minds

QUESTIONS FOR RESTLESS MINDS

Who Chose the Books of the New Testament?

Charles E. Hill

D. A. Carson,
Series Editor

LEXHAM PRESS

Who Chose the Books of the New Testament?
Questions for Restless Minds, edited by D. A. Carson

Copyright 2022 Christ on Campus Initiative

Lexham Press, 1313 Commercial St., Bellingham, WA 98225
LexhamPress.com

Print ISBN 9781683595199
Digital ISBN 9781683595205
Library of Congress Control Number 2021937709

Lexham Editorial: Todd Hains, Abigail Stocker, Jessi Strong, Mandi Newell
Cover Design: Brittany Schrock
Interior Design: Abigail Stocker
Typesetting: Justin Marr

The Christ on Campus Initiative exists to inspire students on college and university campuses to think wisely, act with conviction, and become more Christlike by providing relevant and excellent evangelical resources on contemporary issues.

Visit christoncampuscci.org.

Contents

Series Preface

D. A. CARSON, SERIES EDITOR

THE ORIGIN OF this series of books lies with a group of faculty from Trinity Evangelical Divinity School (TEDS), under the leadership of Scott Manetsch. We wanted to address topics faced by today's undergraduates, especially those from Christian homes and churches.

If you are one such student, you already know what we have in mind. You know that most churches, however encouraging they may be, are not equipped to prepare you for what you will face when you enroll at university.

It's not as if you've never known any winsome atheists before going to college; it's not as if you've never thought about Islam, or the credibility of the New Testament documents, or the nature of friendship, or gender identity, or how the claims of Jesus sound too exclusive and rather narrow, or the nature of evil. But up until now you've probably thought about such things within the shielding cocoon of a community of faith.

Now you are at college, and the communities in which you are embedded often find Christian perspectives to be at best oddly quaint and old-fashioned, if not repulsive. To use the current jargon, it's easy to become socialized into a new community, a new world.

How shall you respond? You could, of course, withdraw a little: just buckle down and study computer science or Roman history (or whatever your subject is) and refuse to engage with others. Or you could throw over your Christian heritage as something that belongs to your immature years and buy into the cultural package that surrounds you. Or—and this is what we hope you will do—you could become better informed.

But how shall you go about this? On any disputed topic, you do not have the time, and probably not the interest, to bury yourself in a couple of dozen volumes written by experts for experts. And if you did, that would be on *one* topic—and there are scores of topics that will grab the attention of the inquisitive student. On the other hand, brief pamphlets with predictable answers couched in safe slogans will prove to be neither attractive nor convincing.

So we have adopted a middle course. We have written short books pitched at undergraduates who want arguments that are accessible and stimulating, but invariably courteous. The material is comprehensive enough that it has become an important resource for pastors and other campus leaders who devote their energies to work with students. Each book ends with a brief annotated bibliography and study questions, intended for readers who want to probe a little further.

Lexham Press is making this series available as attractive print books and in digital formats (ebook and Logos resource). We hope and pray you will find them helpful and convincing.

POLITICS

IN THE ONGOING interaction of Christianity with its surrounding culture, the issue of how we got the Bible has become one of the flashpoints of our day. The popular narrative that has sprung up and taken root has become so often repeated, so widely adopted, and its explanatory power has become so effective, that it could probably now qualify as one of our cultural myths: a grand story that serves to explain for a culture a set of phenomena important for its self-understanding. Such a grand story must be simple in its broad strokes, but have enough historical correspondence to make itself plausible to great numbers of people.

Why is such a story about how we got the Bible needed as part of our cultural mythology? That Christianity and its Bible have played a highly prominent role in the history of Western culture is obvious and unavoidable to anyone who studies history. In times when the influence of Christianity is not so seriously questioned, the need for an explanatory myth is perhaps not felt so strongly. But today many would see the cultural landscape quite differently, regarding the remaining effects of Christianity as the final flickerings of a failed human experiment, already in its twilight hours.[1] Our culture apparently needs a myth, then, not to account for its distinctively Christian character, but to explain its one-time fascination with an increasingly discredited religion. It needs to explain how it was that Christianity—not Islam, Judaism, or Hinduism, not secular Humanism or Atheism, but *Christianity*—came to play the elemental role it has in Western, and particularly in American, culture.

ENCOUNTERS WITH THE CULTURAL MYTH

The simple and popular form of the myth is perhaps stated no better than the way Dan Brown gives it in a conversation in *The Da Vinci Code*.

> "Who chose which gospels to include?" Sophie asked
> "Aha!" Teabing burst in with enthusiasm. "The fundamental irony of Christianity! The Bible, as we know it today, was collated by the pagan Roman emperor Constantine the Great."[2]

So, Constantine chose the New Testament books.

I've become fond of telling how a professor in one of my son's classes at the University of Florida asked his students, almost in passing, if anyone knew who it was that chose the books of the Bible? One student's answer fully satisfied his instructor: "The people with the biggest army." So, the people with the biggest army chose the New Testament books—and indeed, Constantine would have had the biggest army at the time, since (as we know from *Star Wars* historians) Supreme Chancellor Palpatine's Imperial storm-troopers had left the scene long, long ago.

People on airplanes, people at Starbucks, tell me the same story or some version of it. It was Constantine who was the key "chooser," and he and the bishops he assembled for the Council of Nicaea in AD 325 (backed, of course, by the biggest army) assembled the Bible as we know it today. Others who have dug a bit deeper, perhaps read a book or taken a college course, may put a finer point on it and say that it was really Athanasius, bishop of Alexandria, who in the year 367 was the first to specify all twenty-seven books of the New Testament.[3] What everyone seems to agree on is that it was a state-sponsored, state-aligned Christianity in the fourth century, fully three centuries after Christ, which chose the New Testament books. The Bible was put together after Christianity had become wedded to the state, and people, societies, and civilizations have been struggling to extract themselves from the perceived entanglements with Christianity and its politically constructed Bible ever since.

Christians who regard the Bible as in any real and transcendent sense the word of God might want to comfort themselves with the thought that this is a myth of Christian origins that has spread only on the popular level, through novels and films, and, yes, the occasional college classroom. Serious scholars and other informed people know it isn't true. The funny thing is that many scholars are sounding a lot like the popularizers. In fact, some of the scholars, like Elaine Pagels of Princeton, Bart Ehrman of the University of North Carolina at Chapel Hill, and others, *are* the popularizers. "The Christian *canonization* process," writes scholar David Dungan in his popular book *Constantine's Bible*, "involved a governmental intrusion into what had been a *scripture selection* process."[4] Dungan regards the Christian creation of a canon of Scripture as "a unique development in the world's religions, found for the first time in fourth- and fifth-century Romanized Catholic Christianity."[5]

There is of course a long history between the time of Jesus and the critical events of the fourth century, the rise of Constantine, the eventual establishment of Christianity as the state religion, and homogenizing councils like the Council of Nicaea and others. In the minds of many scholars today, the one word that characterizes the entire intervening era perhaps better than any other is the word "diversity" (which, by a curious coincidence, also happens to be one of the most prized cultural values of our own day). Christianity from Jesus to Constantine, you might say, could be described as a very loose and largely unco-ordinated movement of diverse groups with varying theologies, all vying for converts in the Greco-Roman world. Some groups were better organized than others, but no group had a majority; no group—from an objective and purely historical viewpoint—should be said to have had a better claim than any other to being *the* true representative of Jesus and his first followers. In this period we are more to speak of Christianities than of Christianity. What is now commonly referred to as the "proto-orthodox"—a term coined on the belief that there was no such thing as orthodoxy before the fourth century—was merely one of many Christian groups competing for followers.[6]

The climactic point in the grand narrative of the myth is stated by Bart Ehrman:

> In brief, one of the competing groups in Christianity succeeded in overwhelming all the others. This group gained more converts than its opponents and managed to relegate all its competitors to the margins. ... This group became "orthodox," and once it had sealed its victory over all of its opponents, it rewrote the history of the engagement—claiming that it had always been the majority opinion of Christianity, that its views had always been the views of the apostolic churches and of the apostles, that its creeds were rooted directly in the teachings of Jesus. The books that it accepted as Scripture proved the point, for Matthew, Mark, Luke, and John all tell the story as the proto-orthodox had grown accustomed to hearing it.[7]

Scholars like Ehrman cite in this regard the well-worn adage: "It's the winners who write the histories." That is, those who get to write the histories are those who have already won the cultural battle. Thus they write history in a way that favors their own party, and puts any rivals in a bad light. The winners who wrote the histories were biased, often so biased, they couldn't even see their own bias. So, when we read early orthodox writers today, we need to adopt a hermeneutic of suspicion, and read against the grain.

This is what the history books are telling us today. But then, isn't history always written by the winners? And aren't the winners often so enmeshed in the reigning cultural narrative that they can't see their own bias? Which is why we ought to read today's historians with the same sort of critical suspicion as they recommend we apply when reading the ancient writers.

If it is true that the books of the New Testament were chosen and assembled under deep political pressure, only after one version of Christianity had achieved victory over its many rivals, what then? Clearly there are many who see this story as a crippling embarrassment to Christians and as another tool by which to marginalize Christianity today. (The marginalization of Christianity would, by the way, qualify as a political end.) But is this necessarily so? Embarrassing as it may be, it would not defeat or delegitimize Christianity. If the books of the New Testament were assembled by hook and by crook, the books were still assembled, and God, according to Christian theology, was not left out of the process. In fact, as the biblical patriarch Joseph told his brothers who had sold him into slavery and abandoned him, "You meant evil against me; but

God meant it for good, to bring it about that many people should be kept alive, as they are today" (Gen 50:20). If this culturally useful narrative about the formation of the Bible turns out to be accurate, the Christian can still look gratefully and joyfully at the saving message preserved in the New Testament and say, "Constantine and his army may have meant it for evil, but God meant it for good, to bring it about that many people should hear the life-giving voice of Jesus in the books that made it into the New Testament."

The ultimate issue with the political approach, then, is not that it poses some insuperable theological problem for Christianity (as some surely think). The issue is, is it true?

POWER PLAYS
AND CONSPIRACIES

Seeing things through the prism of politics and power, our new cultural myth constructs the story of the Bible's formation as a series of epic struggles over what books would be included in the canon (the group or list of books functioning authoritatively as Scripture in Christian churches).[8] These struggles over books mirrored the larger battle for dominance among the many Christian sects. Examples of how such political maneuvering took place are believed to be plentiful. The great German scholar Walter Bauer found one in the letter known as *1 Clement*, written in the last decade of the first century, through which "Rome succeeded in imposing its will on Corinth."[9] Another example involves Irenaeus of Lyons, a man surely not known for his celebration of theological diversity, who wrote in the late second century. Elaine Pagels states categorically that Irenaeus "confronted the challenge" of rival groups "by demanding that believers destroy all those 'innumerable secret and illegitimate writings' that his opponents were always invoking."[10] Again she alludes to Irenaeus's "instructions to congregations about which revelations to destroy and which to keep."[11] It would be a fascinating exercise if we were to list here every passage in which Irenaeus gave instructions about destroying false gospels and other secret revelations and then examine them closely. That is, if we could find those instructions, which we can't, because they don't exist.[12]

The last example is one in which power struggles supposedly ended in the exclusion of certain books. But power plays that brought new books in were going on as well. A favorite one of mine is an early deal, believed by scholars such as Raymond Brown and others to have been struck sometime in the second century between the "Great Church" in Rome and a small, bickering band of renegade churches in Asia Minor. This deal involved adoption of those disputatious churches into the larger fold, and the acceptance of their Gospel, the Gospel of John, a Gospel which these scholars interpret as being itself a political document through and through.[13] Like Irenaeus's campaign of literary destruction, this agreement, though historically certain in the minds of many scholars today, is nowhere found in the annals of recorded history.

Now, knowing what we all know of human affairs, even those in the church, it would seem dangerous to deny that political factors were ever in play in the process of canon formation. And because the stakes were high, it would not be entirely surprising if truth sometimes became a casualty, on every side. Even the "good guys"—however one perceives who they were—were not immune to human foibles. The problem is, first of all, that instances where books were included or excluded to enhance someone's power base are terribly hard to find and substantiate historically. In fact, one could make the case that one reason it took so long to achieve consensus among the churches was precisely because of the deference paid to individual churches to maintain their own local traditions, even in the face of a desire for "catholic" unity. Second, scholars who see things through the prism of politics and power struggles[14] sometimes outrun the evidence and imagine things to have occurred in the way they think they must have occurred. And one could be forgiven for wondering whether there are not often political motives afoot here as well.

Moreover, this approach seems prone to a conspiracy mentality. As we have seen, the assessment of many today is that the orthodox, once they had won the battle, rewrote history, making it look like their views had always been the majority views in the church. Not only did they rewrite history but they must have colluded to wipe out traces of the actual history. For, given that Christianity before the fourth century is supposed to have been a lively assortment of diverse factions with no mainstream, if one questions why it is that the vast majority of Christian writings surviving from the second and third centuries seem to embody this one proto-orthodox stream, rather than Marcionite, Valentinian, Ophite, etc., the answer is simple. The once-plentiful literature of the many rival groups was suppressed and eliminated by the one victorious party. What Pagels accuses Irenaeus of doing to his rivals' holy books on a small scale, later Christian leaders of the fourth and fifth centuries are thought to have done on a more massive scale. One could account for most of the lack of evidence in a less conspiratorial way, simply by recognizing that the great bulk of heretical literature simply died away through attrition (as did the bulk of orthodox literature) and was not replaced. Naturally, it is the literature useful to the victors that was most likely to be preserved and recopied over the centuries, once orthodox Christianity and its scholars held a tolerated and then a favored position with the state. But many are not satisfied with such innocent explanations.[15]

THE PROOF IS IN THE PAPYRI?

Proof of Christianity's once-prevailing diversity and of the efforts of later Christians to rewrite the history is often believed to reside in the discoveries of early Christian papyri.[16] These are the exciting archaeological finds, like the *Gospel of Judas*, or more recently in 2012 the so-called *Gospel of Jesus' Wife*, that seem to pop up with regularity, especially right before Christmas and Easter. In 2004, noting the existence of a relatively large number of extracanonical Christian writings unearthed at the famous site of Oxyrhynchus, Egypt, Eldon J. Epp wrote, "The collocation with our so-called 'New Testament' papyri of such recognized or possible candidates for canonicity raises serious issues, such as the propriety of designating *two* categories of writings in this early period: 'New Testament' and 'apocryphal....'"[17] Not only are "New Testament" and "apocryphal" writings found at the same archaeological sites, some scholars see the latter as outnumbering the former. When the *Gospel of Judas* was published in 2006, Ehrman stated it bluntly: "Amazingly," he wrote, "virtually every time a new document is found, it is 'heretical' rather than 'proto-orthodox.'"[18]

With the "artifactual" evidence in mind, Epp continued in his 2004 article, "there is no basis ... to claim that the 'New Testament' manuscripts stand out as a separate or separable group" from the others.[19] In other words, the dispassionate and impartial discoveries of archaeology are thought to show us what was really happening, on the ground, despite what biased theologians like Irenaeus, Origen, or Eusebius might have wanted their readers to believe. Prior to the fourth century, in the view of many scholars writing today, Christian literature was flowing freely and believers were making no distinctions between books like the Gospel of John and the *Gospel of Mary*, Paul's letter to the Romans, and the letter of Ptolemy the Valentinian to a woman named Flora.

What should we say about the archaeological discoveries? One of the first things we should say is that there is always a temptation to generalize too much from randomly discovered archaeological evidence. Such evidence has the advantage of being unbiased, but the disadvantage of being haphazard and largely in need of context. And yet, there is certainly a great deal to be gained from this important and growing body of artifactual evidence. Here I would like to summarize our current state of that evidence, focusing on the Gospels.[20]

We have four Gospels we now call canonical. Scholars point out, from references to other gospels found in surviving literature, that there may have been eight or ten or maybe even twelve other gospels circulating in the second and third centuries, so, two to three times as many non-canonical as canonical ones. But simply estimating the number of gospels in existence does not tell us how many people or churches were using each one, or for what purposes they might have been using them. Currently, archaeologists have dug up *ten* fragments from one of the maybe eight to twelve non-canonical gospels dated to the second or third centuries. The number of fragments of one of the four canonical Gospels from the same period is about *forty*, so a ratio of four to one. This suggests that, even though there were more alternative gospels than canonical Gospels in existence, apparently these others weren't being copied and circulated as much as the four. But this only tells us part of the story.

Is it really the case that there is nothing that differentiates the canonical from the non-canonical ones? (See Figure 1.)

Figure 1. Two Early Gospel Fragments

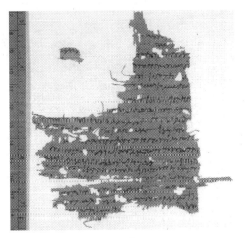

Gospel A   Gospel B

One does not need to know one iota of Greek in order to see that there is a clear, visible difference between these two contemporary gospel fragments from the third century. Gospel A exhibits a rapidly-written, informal, cursive hand, the kind customarily used for bills of sale and other documentary records. This copy of the *Gospel of Mary* (P. Oxy. 3525) was clearly intended for private and not for public reading.

Gospel B is written in a clear, upright, very regular, even calligraphic hand, an early example of a formal book hand often called "biblical majuscule." The scribe, clearly a professional, produced a formal and easily-readable transcription. This copy of the Gospel of John (P. Oxy. 1780 also known as P[39]) was almost certainly intended for public reading, no doubt in a gathering for worship.

This comparison is a bit extreme: most early manuscripts of canonical writings are not so well-executed as this copy of John, and most non-canonical manuscripts are not as sloppy as this copy of the *Gospel of Mary* (although there is no early, non-canonical gospel manuscript so "high-class" as P[39]). I've selected these two examples to illustrate the simple point that there can be and often are clear differences between manuscripts, differences which can suggest quite different circumstances of manufacture and differences in intended use. And perhaps more important than the obvious difference between these two in the care and skill in writing is something you cannot see from the photographs: Gospel A (P. Oxy. 3525, *Gospel of Mary*)[21] is written on a roll, Gospel B (P[39], Gospel of John)[22] on a codex.

Why is this important? For whatever reason, early Christians chose to copy their Scriptural books, both Old Testament and New Testament books, into codices (with pages, like a modern book) rather than onto the more common format of a roll or scroll. There are only a few New Testament manuscripts that are written on the *back* side of used rolls (these are called opisthographs), a practice adopted probably when other writing materials were scarce or unaffordable. Of the forty or so pre-fourth century representations of one of the four Gospels, not one is copied onto an unused roll. Only one is an opisthograph. By comparison, of the ten non-canonical gospel fragments, only *five* are in codex form. This means that, currently, in 50 percent of the cases, there is indeed something that distinguishes contemporary non-canonical gospels from canonical ones: *their basic physical form.* (See Figure 2.)

Figure 2. Formats of Second and Third Century
Gospel Manuscripts

Gospel	Unused Roll	Opisthograph	Codex
Matthew	o	o	13
Mark	o	o	1
Luke	o	o	7
John	o	1	18
Thomas	1	1	1
Mary	1	o	1
Peter	1	o	o
"Egerton"	o	o	1
"Fayum"	1	o	o
P.Oxy.4009	o	o	1
P.Oxy.5072	o	o	1

Further, those five non-canonical gospels that are left, that were copied into codices, tend to lack other physical or scribal characteristics that set almost all the New Testament manuscripts off from others. These characteristics include careful handwriting, as we saw above, but also standard codex size, and the use of readers' aids like punctuation, paragraphing, and the like.[23] It comes down to one or maybe two that have even the same outward form and basic scribal characteristics comparable to the mainstream of canonical-Gospel productions. That is before we even talk about their contents, which, in most cases, is where the real differences begin!

This suggests either that the scribes who copied canonical and non-canonical gospels either belonged to different socio-religious groups or scribal networks, or if they were in the same groups or networks, they were making conscious distinctions between Scriptural and non-Scriptural documents, even at the stage of copying.

Now, one of the most significant things about the evidence just cited is that all the papyri we have been talking about are dated to the period *before* the establishment of Christianity in the fourth century. That means they all come from a time before there could have been any suppression of competing gospels by state-sponsored Christianity.

Another point of interest is that the papyri all come from Egypt. Why is this important? Egypt is consistently portrayed by historians of early Christianity as the hotbed of alternative Christianities in the early period. "Heterodoxy," says Epp, "was the mark of the earliest Egyptian period."[24] Ehrman concurs: "the earliest Christians in Egypt were

18

various kinds of gnostic."[25] Even if these statements are somewhat exaggerated, no historian would deny that the tide of theological diversity in the second and early third centuries was perhaps at its highest in Egypt. What that means is that if there is any place in the Mediterranean world where we should expect the "heterodox" Christian books to outnumber "orthodox" ones, it is in Egypt. The fact that heterodox gospels do not even come close to doing so (even some of the non-canonical gospels are probably not heterodox), that they are in fact currently outnumbered four to one, and that most of them have distinctively different physical properties from the canonical Gospels are, I think, ponderous problems for the political interpretation.

2

PRAXIS

W HILE THE POLITICAL approach just described seems to have emerged as the dominant one both in academia and especially in the popular culture—so much so that it has contributed to our current cultural mythology—it is also fair to say that not all scholars of early Christianity are driven towards primarily political explanations. These scholars realize that churches were mostly busy with their own internal affairs: corporate gatherings for worship, instruction, and fellowship; mission and evangelism; inter-church relations; cultural engagement of various kinds, including, in many instances, trying to avoid harassment or martyrdom. Churches were not fixated on the effort to eliminate rival Christian groups. Even those scholars who favor political explanations usually give some attention to other factors leading to the construction of the Bible as we know it. Key among those factors was the alleged development of certain criteria of canonicity applied to the books available.

One of the most widely-published writers on the for-mation of the New Testament canon working today is Lee McDonald. McDonald reports that it is generally acknowl-edged among scholars "that the churches used several cri-teria, often unequally, in order to determine the contents of their New Testament."[26] As these scholars see it, the churches needed "guidelines ... to determine which books were to be included in their scripture collections and which were not."[27] "The most common criteria employed in the process," McDonald says, "include apostolicity, orthodoxy, antiquity, and use," with the last one being the most determinative.[28] He offers the following explanations:

> The writings eventually incorporated into the New Testament apparently met the worship and instructional needs of the churches, while the others did not. The writings that did not remain in the church's sacred collections were those that did not meet the needs of the greater church and had more difficulty being adapted to the churches' changing needs.[29] ...
>
> Ultimately, it appears that the writings that were accorded scriptural status were the ones that best conveyed the earliest Christian proclamation and that also best met the growing needs of local churches in the third and fourth centuries.[30] ...
>
> The key to understanding the preservation and canonization of the books which make up our current New Testament is probably usage, especially usage in the larger churches during the third through the fifth centuries.[31]

This model tends to picture the churches as faced with a nearly undifferentiated mass of similarly-credentialed books, and applying to these books a number of tests: "is it apostolic? Is it orthodox? Is it ancient? Do we find it useful?" Compared to the political approach, especially in any of its more extreme, popular forms, the emphasis here might seem more reasonable, and more appealing. It is only common sense that the church should authorize—canonize—the books it found most *useful*, those that ministered to its membership in worship, preaching, catechizing, counseling, and conversation. And it is undeniable that the early church also regarded its New Testament Scriptures as *apostolic* (either written by an apostle or by an apostolic assistant, like Luke or Mark), as *orthodox* (consistent with the witness of the rest of the Scriptures and the church's creedal expressions), and as *catholic* (valid for and recognized in not just one localization of the church but across its broad expanse). Yet, there are also empirical problems with this way of conceiving of the canon as the result of the churches' "praxis," its practice of using a set of criteria for determining its authoritative Scriptures.

First, scholars who stress the role of criteria usually characterize what happened as a selection process and try to deduce what criteria churches used in that process. Yet we do not find in the ancient writers any lists of criteria, or any discussions of criteria for *selecting* books. That is, while Scriptural books are sometimes explicitly acknowledged to be (among other things) apostolic, orthodox, and catholic, and other books might not be, there is no evidence that the books used as Scripture by the church had first been subjected to a list of qualifying criteria before they were used and acknowledged as Scripture.[32] We simply find them being used as such. And if objections to such use arise, or in the case of a newcomer, if a book is put forward to be treated as Scripture, then points might be made in response about its having or not having certain qualities that Scriptural books manifest themselves to have. And for most of the books of the New Testament, there is no suggestion that any tests were applied at all.

Second, all these criteria are considered to have arisen from the mind(s) of the churches, of the second or third centuries, according to their perceived needs. This ignores any inherent, transcendent or divine properties of the books themselves. It assumes that the idea of a set of authoritative, specifically Christian Scriptures was a late idea and far from the intention of Jesus, the apostles, or any of the actual Scriptural authors. We'll come back to this issue later on.

Third, if the church kept only what it thought "met its changing needs," where is the place for God's disruptive, admonitory voice, for "correction and reproof" as Paul says Scripture gives (2 Tim 3:16)? Left to decide for itself, is it likely the church would have chosen the dire warnings and condemnations of some of its tendencies, such as are contained in many New Testament books? For instance, the book of Revelation contains charges levelled by the risen Christ against most of the seven churches it addresses and it threatens dreadful judgment against them. The charges include the sins of abandoning love, tolerating immorality, and the eating of food sacrificed to idols. Paul's letters to the Corinthian church reveal that some of its members were engaged in immoral behaviors, were mistreating each other, or were denying basic tenets of the faith. Some in the Galatian churches were toying with what Paul called a desertion of God and an exchange of the true gospel for a false one. None of these are things any church would want to advertise about itself to other churches or to outsiders in a permanent collection of Scriptures. And who would want to put oneself under a continual threat of divine judgment for misbelief or misbehavior?

Fourth, if use is the key criterion, we cannot account for the acceptance of books like James or Jude, or even an "acknowledged Pauline" book like Philemon, books which, if we had to judge by our current evidence, were not used all that often. As far as we know, there was never any controversy about Philemon, but it is hardly ever cited or mentioned in the early church (not entirely surprising because it is so short). Even McDonald has to concede that some New Testament books "were not cited or used as often as such noncanonical sources as 1 *Clement*, the *Shepherd of Hermas*, the *Didache*, *Barnabas*, and the *Epistles* of Ignatius, and possibly also the *Martyrdom of Polycarp*."[33] I think McDonald may have gotten a little carried away here, but the underlying point is true.

Scholars see this as a simple case of *inconsistency*.[34] The church couldn't even be consistent in applying its own criteria! So, it is a problem for the canon. Instead, scholars should see it as a problem for their method. Rather than calling into question the legitimacy of the books in the church's canon, this "inconsistency" calls into question the idea that the church was using a set of criteria to determine the books in the canon.

For one thing, this approach tends to glide over the fact that some books were valued and used for different purposes. Some were seen as useful for catechetical training or simply for good Christian reading, but were not Scripture. According to our current artifactual evidence, one of the most popular Christian writings in the early church was *The Shepherd of Hermas*. More early fragments of this work have been found than of almost any New Testament book, excepting John and Matthew! The late second-century author of the *Muratorian Fragment* says this about *The Shepherd of Hermas*: "it ought indeed to be read; but it cannot be read publicly to the people in church."[35] This apparently mirrored the attitude of many Christian writers, including Irenaeus,[36] who saw it as quite useful, but not as Scripture—except for Tertullian, who condemned it as apocryphal and false.[37] In the fourth century, Athanasius would call it catechetical but not canonical.[38]

3

PROOF

ONE IMPORTANT THING the political and the practical approaches have in common is that they both perceive the process of selecting the books of the New Testament as the collective act of the church, pure and simple. It may have been a drawn-out battle, full of fractious debates and government coercion. Or it may have been an honest but tedious, evolving process of finding consensus through the inconsistent application of more-or-less legitimate criteria. It may even have been, as many would assert, the authoritative declaration of a particular church hierarchy. But in any case, it was in the church that the idea arose, and it was the church—particularly the church of the fourth and fifth centuries—that spoke with the defining voice.[39]

Any way you slice it, this seems problematic for evangelicals and for historic Protestantism, those who do not believe in an infallible church. How can we place ultimate confidence in a list of books chosen by the church, unless the church too is infallible, at least on par with Scripture or above it in authority? Thus for some, the study of canon has seemed to lead toward Rome, and the Roman Catholic way of looking at things. Since no Scriptural book gives us a list of Scriptural books, how do we know what that list is, unless the church tells us?

SELF-ATTESTING,
SELF-DEMONSTRATING

This was a burning issue at the time of the Reformation, when reform efforts were necessarily focused upon the ultimate source of authority in the church. Was that ultimate divine authority to be sought in Scripture above all else, or was even Scripture's divine voice subject to the church? Calvin refers to those in his day who asked, "Who can assure us that Scripture has come down whole and intact even to our very day? Who can persuade us to receive one book in reverence but to exclude another, unless the church prescribe a sure rule for all these matters? What reverence is due Scripture and what books ought to be reckoned within its canon depend, they say, upon the determination of the church."[40] Calvin and other Protestant theologians answered that the consensus voice of the church is indeed a legitimate and powerful support, once we have faith in the Scriptures. But our confidence in the Scriptures ultimately rests not on human testimony, even the testimony of the church, but on the testimony of God himself by the Holy Spirit, speaking in the Scriptures. The Scriptures are *autopistoi*—self-authenticating, self-attesting, and this extended to the question of canon as well.[41] Calvin put it memorably,

> As to their question—How can we be assured that this has sprung from God unless we have recourse to the decree of the church?—it is as if someone

asked: Whence will we learn to distinguish light from darkness, white from black, sweet from bitter? Indeed, Scripture exhibits fully as clear evidence of its own truth as white and black things do of their color, or sweet and bitter things do of their taste.[42]

Those whom the Holy Spirit has inwardly taught truly rest upon Scripture, and that Scripture indeed is self-authenticated; hence, it is not right to subject it to proof and reasoning.[43]

The key word in the last clause is "subject." As Calvin explains,

Unless this certainty, higher and stronger than any human judgment, be present, it will be vain to fortify the authority of Scripture by arguments, to establish it by common agreement of the church, or to confirm it with other helps. ...[44] Conversely, once we have embraced it devoutly as its dignity deserves, and have recognized it to be above the common sort of things, those arguments—not strong enough before to engraft and fix the certainty of Scripture in our minds—become very useful aids.[45]

What do we say about such an approach? Some will find it instinctively satisfying while others might think of it rather as a clever subterfuge. What I'd like to say here is that Calvin's view, whether he knew it or not, was surprisingly ancient.[46] In the second and early third centuries, well before the historian can speak of a *final consensus* in the church, and before there was any centralized church hierarchy that could even claim the prerogative of determining the books in Scripture, Christian thinkers were speaking of Scripture in tones that sound surprisingly "Protestant."

This comes through most clearly not in intra-Christian discussion or debate (there were no Protestant-Catholic ecumenical dialogues) but in the encounters between Christians and their critics in educated Greco-Roman society. In the competitive and sometimes treacherous marketplace of ideas in the Greco-Roman world, a persistent indictment lobbed at Christianity was its apparent lack of verification. *Apodeixis* (from which we get our word "apodictic"), meaning proof or demonstration, is the main term used. For people like the famous second-century physician and philosopher Galen, Christianity was contemptible for its inability or unwillingness to demonstrate its teachings on philosophical grounds. Galen saw Jews and Christians as believing on the basis of unproved assertions.[47] Some Christians ventured into the fray, interacting with the philosophical objections of the time in their efforts to present the claims of Christ to both Jews and Greeks.

The first of these is a man whose name is lost to posterity. We know him only from a report of an encounter he had late in life with a much younger man, a student of Greek philosophy named Justin, later known as Justin Martyr due to his death by martyrdom in about 165 CE. In Justin's report of this meeting, the old man introduced the young philosopher to the Hebrew prophets, who, he declares, "did not make their statements by means of proof seeing that they were trustworthy witnesses of the truth above all proof."[48]

To his own astonishment, when Justin turned his attention from the Greek philosophers to the Hebrew prophets, he found it to be as the old man had said.[49] He read not only the prophets but also those whom he calls "the friends of Christ" and put his faith in the crucified one.

When later arguing with Trypho, a Jew, Justin constantly finds "proofs" for his Christian views in the Jewish Scriptures, Scriptures that Justin and Trypho held in common.[50] Typical is *Dialogue* 57.4, where Justin offers to collect "proofs" on a topic, and then proceeds simply to quote and recap Scriptural passages from Genesis and Exodus. Or *Dialogue* 39.7–8, where we hear Trypho acknowledge: "For that the messiah suffers and comes again in glory and will receive eternal kingship over all peoples, all of whom will be subjected to his rule, this has been sufficiently proven[51] by you from the aforementioned scriptures. But that this man [Jesus] is he, prove to us. And I replied, 'It has been proven already, gentlemen, to those who have ears.'" Justin's reply shows his understanding that recognizing the truth of self-attesting Scripture requires the work of the Spirit, who gives ears to hear.

But for Justin, there were other writings, besides the writings of the Old Testament prophets, which conveyed the same divine power. Justin testifies that Jesus' words, in the Gospels or *Apostolic Memoirs*, "possess a certain awe in themselves, and are able to put to shame those who turn aside from the straight path; while the sweetest rest is afforded those who diligently practice them."[52] Justin also refers to "God's voice spoken by the apostles of Christ"[53] and to "the mighty word which his apostles ... preached everywhere."[54] In effect, this reflects the familiar division of the New Testament writings between "Gospel" and "the apostles."

To Justin and the old man, the words of Jesus, his apostles, and the prophets, particularly their predictive words that came true in history, were the highest form of proof.[55] Thus Justin is keen to testify that Christians have not "believed empty fables, or undemonstrated words but words filled with the Spirit of God and big with power, and flourishing with grace".[56] The words of Scripture, given by the Spirit of God, had a divine power in and of themselves, even if full recognition of that apodictic power came only to those equipped by the Spirit to hear.

Snyder believes "Justin's use of proof language appears to be one of his signal contributions to the development of early Christian intellectual discourse."[57] Justin and his evangelizer, however, were not the only Christians who thought this way. Near the end of the second century Clement of Alexandria (ca. 145–215) would join the conversation about justifying proof. Borrowing a concept from Aristotle in order to counter Aristotelian objections to Christianity, Clement speaks of God and of Scripture as a "first principle," something that is true by necessity, though itself indemonstrable through logical proofs.

> If a person has faith in the divine Scriptures and a firm judgment, then he receives as an irrefutable demonstration the voice of the God who has granted him those Scriptures. The faith no longer requires the confirmation of a demonstration. "Blessed are those who without seeing have believed" (John 20:29).[58]

Clement later expands on the idea.

> For in the Lord we have the first principle of instruction, guiding us to knowledge from first to last ... through the prophets and the gospel and the blessed apostles. And, if any one were to suppose that the first principle stood in need of something else, it could no longer be really maintained as a first principle. He then who of himself believes the Lord's Scripture and his actual voice is worthy of belief. ... Certainly we use it [Scripture] as a criterion for the discovery of the real facts. But whatever comes into judgment is not to be believed before it is judged, so that what is in need of judgment cannot be a first principle. With good reason therefore having apprehended our first principle by faith without proof, we get our proofs about the first principle *ex abundanti* from the principle itself, and are thus trained by the voice of the Lord for the knowledge of the truth. ...

We do not wait for the witness of men, but we establish the point in question by the voice of the Lord, which is more to be relied on than any demonstration or rather which is the only real demonstration.[59]

In tune with Justin and Clement is an anonymous author of the second or third century who began his treatise on the resurrection this way:

The word of truth is free, and carries its own authority, disdaining to fall under any skilful argument, or to endure scrutiny through proof by its hearers. But it would be believed for its own nobility, and for the confidence due to him who sends it. Now the word of truth is sent from God; wherefore the freedom claimed by the truth is not arrogant. For being sent with authority, it were not fit that it should be required to produce proof of what is said; since neither is there any [proof] beyond itself, which is God. For every proof is more powerful and trustworthy than that which it proves. ... But nothing is either more powerful or more trustworthy than the truth.[60]

Again, Scripture, the word of truth, because it comes from God, carries with it its own authority and does not depend on the skillful proofs of men. I cite one last expression of the theme, this one from Origen in his great work against Celsus written ca. 246, who traces this way of thinking back to its apostolic source.

> We have to say, moreover, that the Gospel has a demonstration of its own, more divine than any established by Grecian dialectics. And this diviner method is called by the apostle the "demonstration of the Spirit and of power" (1 Cor 2:4).[61]

It was Paul who testified to the Corinthians that his speech and message "were not in plausible words of wisdom, but in demonstration of the Spirit and of power" (1 Cor 2:4), who reported that his gospel came to the Thessalonians "not only in word, but also in power and in the Holy Spirit and with full conviction" (1 Thess 1:5), accepted "not as the word of men but as what it really is, the word of God, which is at work in you believers" (1 Thess 2:13).

The old man, Justin, Clement of Alexandria, the author of *On the Resurrection*, and Origen were not only testifying to their own experience of Scripture as the self-demonstrating Word of God, they were echoing the self-testimony of Scripture's authors themselves.

I've taken the time to reproduce the words of these authors for three reasons. First, this aspect of early Christian thought is not well known, but deserves to be. That Christian thinkers, virtually from the birth of what we might call self-consciously Christian, philosophical thought, were treating Scripture as God's self-attesting and self-demonstrating voice suggests the foundational character of this conception. What was revealed in Scripture served as a basis for intellectual discourse. Rather than

41

standing in need of proof, Scripture was proof. Second (and this is probably one reason why this material is not better known), it exposes the deep epistemological chasm that separates the ancients from many of those who study them today in a post-Enlightenment age. To assume that the ancient Christians must have reasoned the way we do is to commit anachronism.

Third, and most immediately relevant for our present purposes, this material is cited here because it provokes some crucial questions: How could people who conceive of Scripture this way, as the self-demonstrating voice of God, presume to judge which books were useful enough to be treated as Scripture and which were not? How could those for whom Scripture was the criterion of truth, apply criteria for truth to Scripture? From what they tell us, there is little reason to think that they did.

Quite in keeping with what we have seen above, early Christian writers of the second and third centuries describe their own actions with regard to the books of Scripture with words like "receiving," "recognizing," and "confessing." Irenaeus criticizes the Marcionites for not "recognizing" certain books of the New Testament, and others because they do not "confess" the Scriptures but pervert them with their interpretations;[62] others because they "do not admit" John's Gospel but "set it aside."[63] The *Muratorian Fragment* names certain books that cannot be "received" into the catholic church.[64] Justin Martyr had earlier spoken of books "confessed" by the Jews and books not "confessed" by them.

The intuitive response of the church is to *receive, confess, adopt* whatever God has graciously given to his people, through his authorized mouthpieces, whether the church finds that these books meet its felt needs or whether they challenge or rebuke its needs. For Scripture, as Paul had written, and as the church discovered through experience, is profitable for teaching, for reproof, for correction, and for training in righteousness (2 Tim 3:16).

NOT CHOSEN BUT INHERITED

Many historians of the canon today tend to envision what happened in something like the following way. It was not until sometime in the second century when churches began to think they needed a new set of Scriptures,[65] and when they did they were already faced with a sprawling assortment of books that had piled up over the years. As there was no effective, centralized hierarchy in the church issuing authoritative decrees on the subject, each church or group of churches in a region would have to start essentially from scratch and construct its own set of authoritative writings. Thus, as we saw above, scholars posit the need for churches to develop sets of criteria. We saw some of the problems with this approach above. Here we consider the idea that such a sorting process began only in the second century with a relatively large body of candidates and was carried out by churches, in various *ad hoc* ways. Here are two problems with such an approach.

First, if this were the case, and particularly if Christianity was as diverse and disorderly as we are led today to believe, we would expect to find considerably diverging sets of writings being cited as Scripture. But this is not what we find. The sets of books used as New Testament Scripture and called Scripture before the late fourth century vary to some degree, but that degree is not especially large.

We could compare, for instance, the two Christian authors from whom we have the most material near the end of the second century, Irenaeus in Lyons and Clement in Alexandria. Despite the common assertion that the notion of a New Testament canon, a closed collection of books, simply did not exist before the fourth century,[66] it appears that Irenaeus, for one, disagreed. In *Against Heresies* 4.33.8 Irenaeus speaks of "the unfeigned preservation, coming down to us, of the scriptures, with a complete collection allowing for neither addition nor subtraction …"[67] This sounds a lot like a closed collection of Scriptures, or, a canon. It must be said, however, that neither Irenaeus nor Clement ever produces for us a full list of his New Testament Scriptures. We can only hope to gain a close approximation of what their New Testaments must have contained by looking at the quotations and statements they make in their writings. When we do this, we can see even from our approximations that these collections were very similar. (See Figure 3.)

Chapter 3 | Proof

Figure 3. The New Testament Collections of
Irenaeus and Clement of Alexandria

	Irenaeus of Lyons	Clement of Alexandria
Gospels	Matthew, Mark, Luke, John	Matthew, Mark, Luke, John
Acts	Acts of the Apostles	Acts of the Apostles
Paul	13 letters	13 letters + Hebrews
Other Letters	Hebrews	
		James
	1 Peter	1 Peter
	2 Peter?	2 Peter
	1 John	1 John
	2 John	2 John
	3 John?	3 John
		Jude
Apocalypses	Apocalypse of John	Apocalypse of John
		Apocalypse of Peter?
Others	Hermas?	Barnabas?
		Hermas?
		Didache?
		1 Clement?
Not Cited	James	
	Jude	

Despite the abundance of Gospels available (remember, experts claim that perhaps 8–12 other Gospels existed), each of these writers confesses only four to be authentic and authoritative—and these were the same four. Each uses the same book of Acts—no apocryphal *Acts of Andrew*,

45

Acts of John, or *Acts of Peter*. Each has apparently the same thirteen epistles of Paul, plus Hebrews, though Clement attributes Hebrews to Paul and Irenaeus gives no indication of its authorship. Each also uses 1 Peter, 1 John, 2 John, and Revelation as Scripture. That is at least twenty-three books of our twenty-seven that the Alexandrian and the Lyonian clearly had in common, and indeed, this group of books appears to be fairly stable throughout the churches of the time.[68] And what about the remaining epistles, James, Jude, 2 Peter, and 3 John?

I think there are traces of the knowledge of both 2 Peter[69] and of 3 John[70] in Irenaeus's writings, though these are not so clear as to be obvious. There is no apparent use of James and Jude. It is not impossible that Irenaeus simply found no reason to cite James or Jude and that he had all twenty-seven books of our New Testament.[71] I would not claim that he did, only to observe that his New Testament, if it was not identical to our own, must have been quite close to it.

As for Clement, he seems to have accepted all of the non-Pauline letters of the New Testament. So, it appears that Clement had all twenty-seven books. The catch is that Clement may have accepted two or three, some say as many as five other books as well (*Ps. Barnabas*, the *Apocalypse of Peter*, *The Shepherd of Hermas*, possibly *1 Clement*, and *Didache*). He certainly used these books and valued them highly, though it is not entirely clear that he considered any or all of them to be Scripture (and I would have particular doubts about the last three).[72]

In any case, the fact that the collections of new Christian Scriptures used by Clement and Irenaeus in the late second century, on opposite sides of the Mediterranean Sea, resemble each other so closely, undermines the notion that churches, at a relatively late date in the second century, were only beginning to sort through a large mass of Christian writings.

To carry the story of these early corpuses or canons further for a moment, already by about the middle of the third century one could say that the ones used by Clement and Irenaeus are coalescing, as is visible in the work of Origen. In his *Homilies on Joshua*, Origen actually gave a list of the New Testament books which corresponds exactly with our own twenty-seven, including James and Jude but no *Barnabas, Shepherd,* or *Apocalypse of Peter*. Some scholars, however, disqualify this list because we have it only in an early fifth-century Latin translation by Rufinus of Aquileia and the original Greek is lost. Besides, Origen reports elsewhere that some of the New Testament books (2 Pet, 2 and 3 John, 2 Tim) were disputed by others. But, as Metzger has suggested, it is entirely understandable that Origen would give his own view in a homily while qualifying his reports in his more scholarly writings.[73] Moreover, the same list of New Testament books is all but established by Origen's use of and comments about them elsewhere.[74]

The textbooks will emphasize that by the time Eusebius wrote his *Ecclesiastical History* in the early years of the fourth century, several of the books of the New Testament were still disputed: Hebrews, James, 2 Peter, 2 and 3 John, and Jude, and by this time, Revelation too had fallen under suspicion in the minds of some, including Eusebius himself. What the textbooks usually bypass is that while Eusebius faithfully reports that these books are disputed by some, he also says they are used by most of the churches.[75] And if you add these disputed books to the group he says are "acknowledged by all," you get a list of exactly our twenty-seven—meaning that according to Eusebius, most churches were using just these twenty-seven, and no other books as their New Covenant Scriptures. This state of affairs in the church owes nothing to Constantine the Great or the Council of Nicaea. And if we take Eusebius's words seriously, it means that when Athanasius in 367 gave a list of the twenty-seven books of the New Testament, he was hardly proposing something novel. On the contrary, he was reproducing what must have been by that time the traditional New Testament of many churches.

Besides the fact that the collections of New Testament Scripture at the end of the second century look very similar, another reason for doubting the idea that the churches began selecting books in the second century by the use of certain criteria, is that these collections did not simply materialize at that time. The writers profess that they had received their Scriptures from past generations. As

Everett Ferguson says, "The early ecclesiastical writers did not regard themselves as deciding which books to accept or reject. Rather, they saw themselves as acknowledging which books had been handed down to them."[76]

In Antioch in the 190s, Bishop Serapion testifies that the pseudonymous *Gospel of Peter* was not among the books he had received from his forebears.[77] This means, of course, that other books *were* in that collection. To judge from the works of Theophilus (see note 68), one of Serapion's immediate predecessors, the New Testament collection or canon in the Antioch church must have included at least the four canonical Gospels, Acts, a corpus of Paul's epistles, and Revelation. At just about the same time, Clement in Alexandria speaks in a similar way about "the four Gospels that have been handed down to us."[78] About a decade earlier, Irenaeus in Gaul had spoken of the Gospels, and other books, as having been handed down to the church.[79] He once contrasts the so-called *Gospel of Truth* to "those [Gospels] which have been handed down to us from the apostles."[80]

In other words, the churches represented by these authors did not see themselves as involved in a process of trying to decide which books, out of the many available, would be most useful for meeting the changing needs of their congregations. It seems quite significant that we encounter not only nearly the same collection of books, but also the same way of perceiving of these books—as handed down from the earliest of times—in geographical regions so far separated from each other as Antioch, Syria; Alexandria, Egypt; and Lyons, Gaul, at roughly the same time.

The terminology used by such writers also illustrates an important social reality. The handing on of authoritative books involved chains of human relationships in the churches. Generations of Christians passed down the holy books, not unlike the way heirlooms might be passed down in a family. Irenaeus claims that the chain goes all the way back to the apostles.

And in Irenaeus's mind, that chain was not very long. As a child, and extending into his late teens and possibly well into his twenties, Irenaeus had sat under the teaching of Polycarp in Smyrna.[81] At that time Polycarp was an elder statesman of the church, but when Polycarp was a young man being nurtured in the faith, several of Jesus' apostles were still alive. According to Irenaeus, Polycarp had been ordained by apostles, and used to recount publically some of the things he had heard from apostles. While we cannot, of course, accept everything that Irenaeus says uncritically, it is at least a good inference that when Irenaeus in the 180s speaks of Gospels and other books handed down from the apostles, he would probably have had in mind the books used in the church of his youth in Smyrna under Polycarp's leadership, perhaps 30–50 years earlier. And in his perception, these books had been in use there even before he was born in about 130. He believed that the apostle John was alive "almost in our day"[82] and was active in the region in which Irenaeus had grown up.[83]

Polycarp himself, in the lone letter preserved under his name, does not mention any personal acquaintance with any apostles, unless it is this: "So, then, let us serve him with fear and all reverence, just as he himself has commanded, as did the apostles who preached the gospel to us."[84] It is entirely possible that by "us" Polycarp is including himself personally.[85] But even if not, Polycarp affirms the indispensable channel by which he and the rest of the church received the gospel: the apostles of Jesus. This same channel is mentioned by Polycarp's older contemporary, Clement of Rome, who, probably in the last decade of the first century, writes,

> The apostles received the gospel *for us* from the Lord Jesus Christ; Jesus the Christ was sent forth from God. So then Christ is from God, and the apostles are from Christ.[86]

This is exactly Irenaeus's view a century later, who writes: "For the Lord of all gave to his apostles the power of the Gospel, through whom also we have known the truth, that is, the doctrine of the Son of God; to whom also did the Lord declare: 'The one who hears you hears me, and the one who rejects you rejects me and him who sent me' (Luke 10:16)."[87] Even though these last quotations do not mention books, they show where the authority lay.

The claim of the churches in the late second century is that they had not chosen their books out of a larger pool of contenders but had *inherited* them through chains of

Christian leaders that were in some cases only a few links away from Jesus' apostles. This claim is not contested by our evidence, as far as it goes, which shows that at least most if not all of our New Testament books were in use from the time of their first circulation to the late second century, and beyond. While it may be tempting to write off such claims as either naïve, or duplicitous, or both, their consistency and wide distribution are not so easy to explain.

It is also interesting to note that while so many modern critics dispute or dismiss such claims, ancient critics apparently did not. Celsus, a second-century, pagan opponent of Christianity, accepted that the Gospels went back to Jesus' apostles. So did the advocates of "alternative" Christianities. Valentinians and Gnostics typically did not deny or dispute the church's claims that their books could be attributed to the apostles of Jesus or their companions. Instead, they tried to do them one better, claiming that the apostles "wrote before they had knowledge,"[88] or that what the apostles wrote had been corrupted by the church (Marcion). Some of these groups made great interpretive efforts to use the church's writings and adapt them to their teaching. But the ace they always held up their sleeve was a claim to possess superior knowledge, secret knowledge delivered privately by Jesus to one or two disciples:

- The *Gospel of Judas*, introduces itself as "The secret revelatory discourse in which Jesus spoke with Judas Iscariot."

- The *Gospel of Thomas*, begins, "These are the secret sayings which the living Jesus spoke and which Didymos Judas Thomas wrote down."

- The *Gospel of Mary* has Mary saying to the apostles, "Whatever is hidden from you and I remember, I will proclaim to you."

- The *Apocryphon of James* even depicts the apostles of Jesus writing their books, before it goes on to record a new revelation of Jesus to the apostles after the resurrection.

Here is the point: to trade on *secret* words of Jesus concedes that there are *public* words already well-known, functioning as a kind of standard or criterion. These alternative voices thus in a backhanded way seem to attest to the *mainstream*, orthodox tradition.

The early Christians did not see it as their task to choose the New Testament books. When allowed to speak for themselves, they give no indication of participating in some kind of open application process, in which all candidates—all gospels, epistles or apocalypses claiming apostolic credentials—were invited for submission and given equal consideration. They speak rather of accepting and passing on what had been passed down to them from the apostles, Jesus' commissioned witnesses, those entrusted with the facility to speak by the Holy Spirit in Jesus' name.

4

CONCLUSION

A CULTURE THAT PERCEIVES itself as increasingly post-Christian benefits from a grand narrative, a myth, that can account for its one-time devotion to Christianity and its Bible. But some myths cry out loudly for myth-busting. The books of the New Testament, as it turns out, were not chosen by Constantine, his generals, or the bishops he summoned to Nicaea in AD 325. These twenty-seven books did not gain their authority through the discovery that they were the most effective blunt instruments by which orthodox Christians could thrash their rivals.

Nor is it right to regard the books of the New Testament as simply the survivors of a long and tortuous selection process conducted by churches, either individually or collaboratively, who set out to gather from a wide array of options the best worship and teaching resources to meet its evolving needs. The churches of the second century did not see themselves as authorized to make such selections for themselves.

They saw themselves instead as the favored recipients, preservers, and proclaimers of the life-giving message God had given to the world in Jesus Christ. They believed that Jesus, just as the Gospels and Acts portrayed it, had entrusted that message to a definite group of apostles, who ultimately became the source of a new set of books. In these books the church continued to hear the self-attesting, saving, and abiding voice of God. Even as these books were being written and circulated, communities of Christians were being birthed here and there throughout the known world. Besides the books that emanated from genuine apostolic sources, other books appeared which paralleled, imitated, or supplemented them. The course of historical events that brought consensus to a church so widely distributed and often expanding was neither quick nor especially orderly. But it is important to stress that until that consensus was reached in the fourth century, the church was never without the word of God. At first the apostolic preaching, and then a collection of apostolic books bearing the self-authenticating message of Jesus was functioning all the way through, even if it was sometimes incomplete, and sometimes joined by the voices of other useful books, to provide that word of God for the people of God.

Bruce Metzger, one of the last century's leading scholars of the New Testament canon, had it right, I think, when he observed, "neither individuals nor councils created the canon; instead they came to recognize and acknowledge the self-authenticating quality of these writings, which imposed themselves as canonical upon the church."[89] William Barclay put it more succinctly: "It is the simple truth to say that the New Testament books became canonical because no one could stop them doing so."[90] These historical assessments could well be seen as commentaries on the words Jesus once spoke to a group of his critics: "My sheep hear my voice" (John 10:27).

Acknowledgments

THE SERIES Questions for Restless Minds is produced by the Christ on Campus Initiative, under the stewardship of the editorial board of D. A. Carson (senior editor), Douglas Sweeney, Graham Cole, Dana Harris, Thomas McCall, Geoffrey Fulkerson, and Scott Manetsch. The editorial board recognizes with gratitude the many outstanding evangelical authors who have contributed to this series, as well as the sponsorship of Trinity Evangelical Divinity School (Deerfield, Illinois), and the financial support of the MAC Foundation and the Carl F. H. Henry Center for Theological Understanding. The editors also wish to thank Christopher Gow, who created the study questions accompanying each book, and Todd Hains, our editor at Lexham Press. May God alone receive the glory for this endeavor!

Study Guide Questions

1. Have you thought about who chose the books of the New Testament? Is this something that a non-Christian has asked you? How have you tended to approach this question before reading this book?

2. What are the major views concerning canonization that Hill confronts?

3. What did you learn about the how churches in the second and third centuries thought about Scripture?

4. How would you summarize how the canon came to be recognized in the church?

5. How would you answer if someone asked you how you know the Bible is true?

6. Hill argues that " the church was never without the word of God" (58). What does this mean about the importance of God's word in our own lives? Do your own habits of engagement with Scripture demonstrate that you hold it in high regard?

7. How can you give God's word a more prominent and authoritative role in your life?

For Further Reading

Ferguson, E. "Factors Leading to the Selection and Closure of the New Testament Canon: A Survey of Some Recent Studies." Pages 295–320 in *The Canon Debate*. Edited by L. M. McDonald and James A. Sanders. Hendrickson, 2002.

Very sensible, expert treatment of the issues.

Hill, C. E. *Who Chose the Gospels? Probing the Great Gospel Conspiracy.* Oxford University Press, 2010.

Counters with historical evidence the prevalent idea that the four canonical Gospels were chosen only late and under dubious circumstances

Kruger, M. J. *Canon Revisited: Establishing the Origins and Authority of the New Testament Books.* Crossway, 2012.

Outstanding introduction that analyzes the field and argues for the superiority of the self-authenticating model of the canon.

———. *The Question of Canon: Challenging the Status Quo in the New Testament Debate.* IVP Academic, 2013.

> Excellent work that answers many of the most pressing critical questions about the New Testament canon.

McDonald, L. M., and James A. Sanders, eds. *The Canon Debate.* Hendrickson, 2002.

> Huge collection of recent material on both Old Testament and New Testament canon. A mine of information, highly recommended, though the articles are of uneven quality. Mostly critical, but the editors included a few traditionalist Roman Catholic, Evangelical, and even Jewish scholars. Ferguson's article (see previous page) is highly recommended.

Metzger, B. M. *The Canon of the New Testament: Its Origin, Development, and Significance.* Clarendon, 1987.

> A classic. Expert, conservative, and very learned. Some interesting discussion of the theological issues.

Ridderbos, H. *Redemptive History and the New Testament Scriptures.* 2nd ed. P&R, 1988.

> Perhaps the best (if short) theological treatment of canon available. Shows that the question of canon is essentially an issue of redemptive history not really of church history. Provides an exegetical and theological framework for historical canon studies.

Notes

1. But then, such prognoses of imminent doom for Christianity have been made before, and have always had to be retracted. For an interesting analysis of the current situation, see Ross Douthat, *Bad Religion: How We Became a Nation of Heretics* (Free Press, 2012).

2. Dan Brown, *The Da Vinci Code: A Novel* (Doubleday, 2003), 231.

3. For example, Bart D. Ehrman, *Lost Christianities: The Battles for Scripture and the Faiths We Never Knew* (Oxford University Press, 2003), "The first Christian author of any kind to advocate a New Testament canon of our twenty-seven books and no others was Athanasius, the fourth-century bishop of Alexandria. This comes in a letter that Athanasius wrote in 367 CE—over three centuries after the writings of Paul, our earliest Christian author"—a statement that might be technically true but very misleading, as we shall see later.

4. David L. Dungan, *Constantine's Bible: Politics and the Making of the New Testament* (Fortress, 2007), 133.

5. Dungan, *Constantine's Bible*, 133.

6. Ehrman, *Lost Christianities*, 176, "As a result of this ongoing scholarship, it is widely thought today that proto-orthodoxy was simply one of many competing interpretations of Christianity in the early church. It was neither a self-evident interpretation nor an original apostolic view. ... Indeed, as far back as we can trace it, Christianity was remarkably varied in its theological expressions."

7. Bart Ehrman, "Christianity Turned on Its Head: The Alternative Vision of the Gospel of Judas," in *The Gospel of Judas from Codex Tchacos*, ed. R. Kasser, M. Meyer, and G. Wurst (National Geographic, 2006), 77–120, at 118. A very similarly worded account may be read in Ehrman, *Lost Christianities*, 173, where the view is ascribed to Walter Bauer in his celebrated work *Orthodoxy and Heresy in Earliest Christianity* (1934). Bauer may be seen as one of the "godfathers" of the currently popular political approach to early Christianity. For more on Bauer and his influence, see Andreas J. Köstenberger and Michael J. Kruger, *The Heresy of Orthodoxy: How Contemporary Culture's Fascination with Diversity Has Reshaped Our Understanding of Early Christianity* (Crossway, 2010).

8. This is a simple, rough and ready, definition of the term canon. Scholars today are divided over whether the idea of "canon" must entail the notion of exclusivity—a definite, closed list—or whether it can simply be used for books that function with divine authority in the church, regardless of whether that list is perceived of as closed or not. The exclusivists insist that we not use the word canon for the period before the fourth century, for it is only at that time when we know that the church perceived its list of books as closed. Before the fourth century, they say, Christians did not have a canon but only individual books of "Scripture," perceived to be authoritative and inspired but belonging to an open-ended collection. Though widely used, such a distinction is not really viable. For a fine treatment of the definition issue, one which does not ignore the ontological dimension, see Michael J. Kruger, *The Question of Canon: Challenging the Status Quo in the New Testament Debate* (IVP Academic, 2013), chapter 1.

9. Walter Bauer, *Orthodoxy and Heresy in Earliest Christianity*, second German ed. with added appendices, by Georg Strecker, trans. a team from the Philadelphia Seminar on Christian Origins, ed. Robert A. Kraft and Gerhard Krodel (Fortress, 1971), 194. As Ehrman says, "for Bauer, the internal Christian conflicts were struggles over power,

not just theology. And the side that knew how to utilize power was the side that won," *Lost Christianities*, 175.

10. Elaine Pagels, *Beyond Belief: The Secret Gospel of Thomas* (Random House, 2003), 147–8.

11. Pagels, *Beyond Belief*, 142.

12. For more on Pagels's treatment of Irenaeus in this regard see C. E. Hill, *Who Chose the Gospels? Probing the Great Gospel Conspiracy* (Oxford University Press, 2010), 58–63, and for scholars' treatment of Irenaeus in general, Chapters 2 and 3.

13. Students will find this interpretation, and the view of history it supports, in Raymond Brown, *The Gospel according to John (i–xii)*, Anchor Bible 29 (Doubleday, 1966); Raymond Brown, *The Gospel according to John (xiii–xxi)*, Anchor Bible 29A (Doubleday, 1970); Raymond Brown, *The Community of the Beloved Disciple: The Life, Loves, and Hates of an Individual Church in New Testament Times* (Paulist Press, 1979), and in many others who follow Brown's approach.

14. "Why had the church decided that these texts were 'heretical' and that only the canonical gospels were 'orthodox'? Who made those decisions, and under what conditions? As my colleagues and I looked for answers, I began to understand the political concerns that shaped the early Christian movement," Pagels, *Beyond Belief*, 33.

15. For example, "The struggle between orthodox and heretics, insofar as it was fought in the literary arena, took the form of an effort to weaken the weaponry of the enemy as much as possible. What could not be *completely eliminated* was at least rendered useless, or was suitably altered and then put to one's own use. In plain language, the writings of the opponent were falsified" (emphasis added), Bauer, *Orthodoxy and Heresy*, 160; compare 110. Ehrman, *Lost Christianities*, 217, also blithely throws around the accusation of unnamed orthodox "burning" and "destroying" heretical books. How they would have obtained all these heretical books from their owners is not stated.

16. Papyrus is the paper-like writing material most used by Christians in the early centuries. It was made from the papyrus reed that grew along the Nile.

17. Eldon J. Epp, "The Oxyrhynchus New Testament Papyri: 'Not without Honor except in their Hometown'?," *JBL* 123 (2004): 5–55 at 17.

18. Bart D. Ehrman, *Jesus, Interrupted: Revealing the Hidden Contradictions in the Bible (and Why We Don't Know About Them)* (Harper One, 2009), 215.

19. Epp, "Not without Honor," 18.

20. For more details on early Gospel manuscripts and their implications for the development of the canon, see C. E. Hill, "A Four-Gospel Canon in the

Second Century? Artifact and Arti-fiction," *Early Christianity* 4 (2013): 310–34.

21.   Egypt Exploration Society.

22.   Ambrose Swasey Library, Colgate Rochester Divinity School, Rochester, New York.

23.   For details see Hill, "A Four-Gospel Canon in the Second Century?," 323–32.

24.   Eldon J. Epp, "The Significance of the Papyri for Determining the Nature of the New Testament Text in the Second Century: A Dynamic View of Textual Transmission," in *Gospel Traditions in the Second Century: Origins, Recensions, Text, and Transmission*, ed. W. L. Petersen (University of Notre Dame Press, 1989), 71–103 at 73.

25.   Bart Ehrman, "Christianity Turned on its Head," 118.

26.   Lee Martin McDonald, "Identifying Scripture and Canon in the Early Church: The Criteria Question," in *The Canon Debate*, ed. Lee Martin McDonald and James Sanders (Hendrickson, 2002), 416–39 at 423.

27.   McDonald, "Criteria Question," 424.

28.   McDonald, "Criteria Question," 423. Many other scholars could be cited as emphasizing the criteria, but I'll only list a few: Harry Y. Gamble, *The New Testament Canon Its Making and Meaning* (Fortress, 1985), 67–70, who lists four criteria: apostolicity,

catholicity, orthodoxy, and traditional usage; Bruce
M. Metzger, *The Canon of the New Testament: Its
Origin, Development, and Significance* (Oxford
University Press, 1987), 251–4, who lists three:
conformity to the "rule of faith," apostolicity, con-
tinuous use and acceptance by the church at large;
F. F. Bruce, *The Canon of Scripture* (IVP Academic,
1988), 255–69, who lists six: apostolic authority,
antiquity, orthodoxy, catholicity, traditional use,
and inspiration; Ehrman, *Lost Christianities*, 240–3,
who lists four: antiquity, apostolicity, catholicity,
and orthodoxy.

29. McDonald, "Criteria Question," 432.

30. McDonald, "Criteria Question," 434.

31. McDonald, "Criteria Question," 434.

32. As stated by H. J. de Jonge, in J.-M. Auwers
and H. J. de Jonge, *The Biblical Canons*, BETL
163 (Leuven University Press, 2003), 309–19 at
312–13, "It should be noticed in passing that these
so-called criteria of canonicity were often used,
not to determine *a priori* whether or not a writing
was authoritative, but to justify *a posteriori* the
high respect in which a writing had already been
held for some time past, or the disapproval it had
already incurred." I think de Jonge has it right here,
except that what he noticed "in passing" is actually
a fundamental point.

33. McDonald, "Criteria Question," 433.

34. "In brief, the so-called criteria of canonicity were used with notable flexibility and irritating inconsistency," de Jonge, "The New Testament Canon," 314.

35. Lines 77–8. For an English translation of the full text of the *Muratorian Fragment*, see Metzger, *Canon*, 305–7.

36. See C. E. Hill, "'The Writing which Says ...' *The Shepherd of Hermas* in the Writings of Irenaeus," in *Studia Patristica* 65, vol. 13: *The First Two Centuries; Apocrypha; Tertullian and Rhetoric; From Tertullian to Tyconius*, ed. Markus Vinzent (Peeters, 2013), 127–38.

37. *On Modesty* 10.12

38. *Ep. Fest.* 39

39. Ehrman, *Lost Christianities*, "After Jesus' death, his teachings ... were granted sacred authority by his followers" (233); later "the authoritative writings of his apostles ... were being granted sacred status before the end of the New Testament period" (234). The very way of stating the issue assumes that it is the church that "grants" sacred status to the books. But as we shall see below, the early Christians evidently did not perceive it that way.

40. *Institutes of the Christian Religion* 1.7.1.

41. See the excellent study by Henk van den Belt, *The Authority of Scripture in Reformed Theology: Truth and Trust* (Brill, 2008).

42. *Inst.* 1.7.2.

43. *Inst.* 1.7.5. "For truth is cleared of all doubt when, not sustained by external props, it serves as its own support" (1.8.1).

44. Contrast the words of the Second Vatican Council, "Thus it comes about that the Church does not draw her certainty about all revealed truths from the Holy Scriptures alone. Hence, both Scripture and Tradition must be accepted and honored with equal feelings of devotion and reverence. Sacred Tradition and sacred Scripture make up a single sacred deposit of the Word of God, which is entrusted to the Church," *Dei verbum*, II.9–10, in *Vatican Council II. The Conciliar and Post Conciliar Documents*, ed. Austin Flanner (The Liturgical Press, 1975).

45. *Inst.* 1.8.1.

46. Most likely he did not know it, or only had an inkling. Van den Belt, *The Authority of Scripture*, investigates the question of whether Calvin derived the term *autopistos* from ancient sources, and searches in particular the Aristotelian and Euclidian traditions (71–83), then the church fathers (84–86). He sees little possibility of influence (due mainly to the unavailability of editions of the most relevant fathers in Calvin's day), touching briefly only upon a possible "indirect" influence from Justin Martyr's *Dialogue* 7.2. Herman Bavinck, *Reformed Dogmatics*,

vol. 1, *Prolegomena*, ed. John Bolt, trans. John Vriend (Baker, 2003), 452, is able to claim general patristic support, but only cites a single sentence of Augustine: "canonical scripture is contained by its own fixed boundaries" (Aug., *De bapt.* 2.3.4).

47. H. Gregory Snyder, "The Classroom in the Text: Exegetical Practices in Justin and Galen," in *Christian Origins and Greco-Roman Culture. Social and Literary Contexts for the New Testament,* ed. Stanley E. Porter and Andrew W. Pitts (Brill, 2013), 663–85, at 678, "On the contrary, Galen affirms that authority flows not from a text or the person behind it, but from proper application of the scientific method, which for him, stands upon the pillars of proper reason and careful observation." The closest analogy in Galen's works to the approaches of Jews and Christians is perhaps in the practice he attributes to Chrysippus, who "keeps turning away from scientific proofs … and uses poets, myths, and women for confirmation of his teaching."

48. *Dialogue* 7.2.

49. Justin's experience seems remarkably similar to that of Calvin, who says, "Read Demosthenes or Cicero; read Plato, Aristotle, and others of that tribe. They will, I admit, allure you, delight you, move you, enrapture you in wonderful measure. But betake yourself from them to this sacred reading. Then, in spite of yourself, so deeply will

it affect you, so penetrate your heart, so fix itself in your very marrow, that, compared with its deep impression, such vigor as the orators and philosophers have will nearly vanish. Consequently, it is easy to see that the Sacred Scriptures, which so far surpass all gifts and graces of human endeavor, breathe something divine" (*Inst.* 1.8.1).

50. By the way, we often rightly complain about someone's practice of "proof-texting" from Scripture, simply listing verses without showing how they prove what we think they are proving. But the very fact that Christians proof-text, that is, use Scriptural citations nakedly as sufficient proof for something, is a very significant thing.

51. Here and in the following two sentences Justin uses the word, ἀποδείχνυμι, "prove," the verbal form of the noun ἀπόδειξις.

52. *Dialogue* 8.2, my translation. Speaking of Jesus, and in particular his predictions of suffering on the part of those who believe in him and confess him to be the Christ, Justin concludes "so that it is manifest no word or act of his can be found fault with" (*Dialogue* 35.7).

53. *Dialogue* 109.

54. *1 Apol.* 45.

55. *1 Apol.* 30.1

56. *Dialogue* 9.1

57. Snyder, "The Classroom in the Text," 685.

58. Clement of Alexandria, *Stromateis Books One to Three*, FTC 85, trans. John Ferguson (The Catholic University of America Press, 1991), 2.2.9.6. Greek text of Clement from Otto Stählin, *Clemens Alexandrinus*, vol. 2, *Stromata Buch I–VI*, GCS 15 (J. C. Hinrichs'sche Buchhandlung, 1906).

59. *Stromateis* 7.16.95. Translation, slightly modified, from *Alexandrian Christianity: Selected Translations of Clement and Origen*, ed. Henry Chadwick and J. E. L. Oulton (Westminster John Knox, 1954), 155. Greek from *Clemens Alexandrinus*, vol. 3, *Stromata Buch VII und VIII, Excerpta ex Theodoto, Eclogae Propheticae, Quis Dives Salvetur, Fragmente*, GCS 17, ed. Otto Stählin (J. C. Hinrichs'sche Buchhandlung, 1909).

60. *On the Resurrection* 1.1–6, ANF 1 etc. While previously the author was thought to be Justin Martyr, many scholars now believe the author is Athenagoras of Athens.

61. *CCels.* 1.2.

62. *Against Heresies* 3.12.12.

63. *Against Heresies* 3.11.9.

64. Lines 66–7; compare 82.

65. E.g., Gamble, *The New Testament Canon*, 12; L. M. McDonald, *The Formation of the Christian Biblical Canon* (Hendrickson, 1995), 319, "The NT canon process began in the second century with the recognition of Christian literature as scripture

that was useful for the teaching and mission of the church."

66. Just one recent example would be David Brakke, "Scriptural Practices in early Christianity: Towards a New History of the New Testament Canon," in *Invention, Rewriting, Usurpation: Discursive Fights over Religious Traditions in Antiquity,* ed. Jörg Ulrich, Anders-Christian Jacobsen, and David Bakke (Peter Lang, 2012), 263–80, at 266, "And so it is simply anachronistic to ask of writers of the second century which books were in their canon and which not—for the notion of a closed canon was simply not there." For more early evidence of the existence of such a notion see C. E. Hill, "The New Testament Canon. Deconstructio ad absurdum?" *Journal of the Evangelical Theological Society* 52 (2009): 101–119, esp. 113–17.

67. *Irenaeus of Lyons,* trans. Robert M. Grant (Routledge, 1997), 161.

68. We might compare, for instance, the usage of Theophilus of Antioch, from slightly earlier, and of Tertullian of Carthage from slightly later. Theophilus appears to use the four Gospels, Acts, a Pauline corpus, and the book of Revelation. He may know more, but this is just what we can deduce from his writings that have survived and from testimonies about the ones that did not survive (see Hill,

Who Chose the Gospels?, 90–93; Metzger, *Canon*, 117–19). Tertullian's New Testament contained the four Gospels, Acts, the Pauline epistles, Hebrews (which he attributed to Barnabas), Revelation, and of the general epistles, at least 1 Peter, 1 John, and Jude (Metzger, *Canon*, 157–160).

69. 2 Peter 1:15 seems to be echoed in *Against Heresies* 3.1.1. This is made more credible by the fact that in Irenaeus's region, writing a few years earlier (in 177 or 178), the author of the *Letter of Vienne and Lyons* apparently knows 2 Peter 1:8 (*HE* 5.1.45).

70. 3 John 9–10 in *Against Heresies* 4.26.3.

71. On his use of *The Shepherd of Hermas*, which some believe he considered to be Scripture, see Hill, "'The Writing which Says.'" It appears that Irenaeus valued this work as a faithful exposition of apostolic teaching but not as apostolic or as Scripture.

72. While Clement obviously holds *The Shepherd of Hermas* in esteem, Batovici concludes "it is not always an easy task to grasp the meaning of this esteem" (Dan Batovici, "Hermas in Clement of Alexandria," in *Studia Patristica* 66, vol. 14: *Clement of Alexandria; The Fourth-Century Debates,* ed. Markus Vinzent [Peeters, 2013], 45–51 at 45). Metzger, *Canon*, 134n43, also observes that "Clement does not hesitate to criticize an interpretation given by the author of the *Epistle of Barnabas* (*Paed.* II. X. 3 and *Strom.* II. Xv. 67)." Eusebius

reports that Clement, in his now lost *Hypotyposes*, gave concise comments about all the canonical Scriptures, "not omitting even the disputed books— that is, the Epistle of Jude and the other Catholic Epistles, and the *Epistle of Barnabas*, and the *Apocalypse of Peter*" (Origen's commentary on Matthew as cited in Eusebius, *Church History* 6.14.1). Exactly what Clement said about these books we unfortunately do not know, but the fact that he treated the last three along with the others probably shows his high esteem for them.

73. So Metzger, *Canon*, 140.

74. There is a similar situation in his *Homilies on Genesis* 13.2, where, without listing all their books, he lists all the New Testament authors: "Isaac, therefore, digs also new wells, nay rather Isaac's servants dig them. Isaac's servants are Matthew, Mark, Luke, John; his servants are Peter, James, Jude; the apostle Paul is his servant. These all dig the wells of the New Testament."

75. *Church History* 2.23.24–25; 3.31.6

76. Everett Ferguson, "Factors Leading to the Selection and Closure of the New Testament Canon: A Survey of Some Recent Studies," in *The Canon Debate*, 295–320 at 295–6.

77. *Church History* 6.12.3–6. On Serapion and what he says relative to the *Gospel of Peter*, see Hill, *Who Chose the Gospels?*, 78–93; for more detail, Hill,

"Serapion of Antioch, the *Gospel of Peter*, and a Four Gospel Canon," in *Studia Patristica* XLV, ed. J. Baun, A. Cameron, M. Edwards, and M. Vinzent (Peeters, 2010), 337–42.

78.   *Stromateis* 3.13.93.

79.   *Against Heresies* 3.1.1.

80.   *Against Heresies* 3.11.9.

81.   See C. E. Hill, *From the Lost Teaching of Polycarp: Identifying Irenaeus' Apostolic Presbyter and the Author of* ad Diognetum, Wissenschaftliche Untersuchungen zum Neuen Testament 186 (J. C. B. Mohr [Paul Siebeck], 2006), and an update in Hill, "The Man Who Needed No Introduction. A Response to Sebastian Moll" in *Irenaeus: Life, Scripture, Legacy,* ed. Sara Parvis and Paul Foster (Fortress, 2012), 95–104.

82.   *Against Heresies* 5.30.3. Irenaeus states that John lived in Ephesus until the times of Trajan (*Against Heresies* 3.3.4), who came to the throne in AD 98 and died in 117.

83.   *Against Heresies* 3.3.4.

84.   *To the Philippians* 6.3.

85.   This may have some relationship to the *Epistle to Diognetus* 11.1, where the author says he became a "disciple of apostles." For the evidence that this "epistle" to Diognetus might preserve the words of Polycarp, see Hill, *From the Lost Teaching of Polycarp,* 97–165.

86. *1 Clement* 42.1–2.

87. *Against Heresies,* preface to Book 3.

88. A charge recorded by Irenaeus, *Against Heresies* 3.1.1.

89. Bruce M. Metzger, *The New Testament, Its Background, Growth and Content,* 3rd ed. (Abingdon, 2003), 318.

90. William Barclay, *The Making of the Bible* (Lutterworth, 1961), 78; cited from Metzger, *Canon,* 286.

LEXHAM PRESS

QUESTIONS FOR RES
MINDS

Printed in the United States
by Baker & Taylor Publisher Services